I0084951

HOW TO TRANSFORM YOUR
MINDSET
AND BECOME A SELF-MADE
SUCCESS STORY

GET OUT OF THE TRUCK

HOW TO TRANSFORM YOUR
MINDSET
AND BECOME A SELF-MADE
SUCCESS STORY

IDAN SHPIZEAR

How to Transform Your Mindset and Become a Self-Made Success Story

Copyright © 2020 Idan Shpizear

All rights reserved. No part of this publication may be reproduced, distributed, or transmitted in any form or by any means, including photocopying, recording, or other electronic or mechanical methods, without the prior written permission of the publisher, except in the case of brief quotations embodied in critical reviews and certain other noncommercial uses permitted by copyright law.

ISBN: 978-0-578-81781-1

First Edition

Cover image: © hxdyl - Dreamstime.com
Cover and interior design: Adina Cucicov

CONTENTS

INTRODUCTION

MANY BUSINESS OWNERS dream of one day being that rags-to-riches story that inspires a new generation of entrepreneurs. You might imagine your face on the cover of Forbes, the article inside marveling at how you transformed your humble beginnings into a thriving empire... how your hard work and commitment revolutionized your industry and employed thousands.

Those who only know me by my professional bio tend to think of my story the same way. I grew up working the dirt on my father's farm in Israel. After moving to the U.S., I began the company now known as 911 Restoration with nothing more than an $800 Volvo and a single carpet cleaning machine. Given that 911 Restoration is now listed among *Entrepreneur's* "Fastest Growing Franchises," it would seem that I am exactly what people talk about when they talk about the American Dream. I worked hard, paid my dues, and now I have the success, the house, and the life I always dreamed about.

Stories like mine are what all entrepreneurs have in mind when they set out to build their own business. These are the stories that tell you success is possible for anyone; you don't have to be born into it (I wasn't) and you don't have to have a degree in business (I don't). If you're like most business owners, you probably have your own list of the self-made entrepreneurs who inspire you. Bill Gates, Warren Buffet, Barbara Corcoran... the business world is full of wildly successful people who came from nothing. In fact, as I write this, *nine* of the ten richest people in the world are self-made entrepreneurs.

So, what is the difference between you and the people whose careers you hope to emulate? What is the difference between your business and mine?

Is it luck? Talent? Discipline? Drive?

No. It's one thing and one thing only.

Mindset.

I am not where I am because I am luckier or inherently more talented than you. In fact, if you heard my entire backstory, you'd probably see a lot of yourself in it. I grew up in a family where financial struggle was a part of everyday life. I did poorly in school and eventually moved to America assuming that my journey to success would be much, much easier than it actually was. As a new business owner, I spent 95% of my energy trying to figure out *how* to make money and only 5% actually making it. I lived in a two-bedroom apartment with six other guys. I hoarded MacDonald's cups so I could go back for free refills.

When I grew my business enough to become someone's boss, I made several leadership missteps. I have stuttered my way through staff meetings and allowed my focus to wander off course. I have experienced major financial losses, spread myself too thin, and had to redesign the way I approach my business. I have been imperfect, mistaken, and short-sighted.

As business owners, we tend to look at the successes of others through a limited lens. We think of Bill Gates as "determined" or Warren Buffet as "shrewd." We talk about every rags-to-riches story like it's an overnight success, glossing over the long period of growth and learning that actually determines whether or not a business owner will excel. Did I turn a Volvo and a carpet cleaning machine into a thriving, nationwide company? Sure I did. But it took a solid decade for me to build a story like that. For years, I worked relentlessly to earn my expertise in this field, scraping together a real-world education in home services, marketing, and finances. And even then, I didn't didn't make major strides until I found mentors and speakers who taught me how to approach my business with a mindset of growth and progress.

I have written this book because I believe I am here—that we are all here—to help others evolve, transform, and discover the lives that were meant for them. I have found success and deep fulfillment because the self-made entrepreneurs who came before me were willing to share their own imperfect backstories. They shared the truth of their struggles and the wisdom they gained from it. As a result, I was able to grow my business faster and find more joy in the process. I promised myself long ago that when I "made it," I would share my own insights as a gesture of appreciation for those who had done the same for me.

This book is the fulfillment of that promise. I am offering honesty and insight in the hopes that you can use my experience as a stepping stone in your own journey to success. I am about to pull back the curtain and reveal the messy side of entrepreneurship... the mistakes, backslides, and self-doubt that I—like all business owners—have had to overcome to get where I am. In doing this, I am going to show you how similar you and I are... show you that you can have what I have as long as you learn to cultivate a growth mindset.

I am going to teach you how to naturally see everything around you as an opportunity to improve your skills, expand your insight, motivate your team, and become a more effective entrepreneur.

This transformation will not happen overnight. The process takes time and patience. But it's time and patience well-spent.

You will learn how to stop using your background, shortcomings, and errors to define your potential as an entrepreneur.

You will finally break the bad mental habits that keep you from earning what you're worth.

You will discover how quickly one small change snowballs into rapid growth and success.

Above all, you will stop seeing yourself as a victim of professional challenges and start seeing yourself as a self-made entrepreneur who has complete control over the fate of his business.

Your mindset determines your ability to succeed more than any business strategy ever will. It is the most powerful tool at your disposal. Believe me. When the 2008 Recession hit, I lost almost everything. My business was struggling, I lost all my real estate investments, and my wife and I weren't even sure how we were going to pay our mortgage.

The only thing that helped me overcome and thrive was the realization that my failings were not a reflection of bad luck. They were a reflection of the chaos inside my mind.

If I wanted more positivity and fulfillment in my life, I had to begin by finding positivity and fulfillment within.

I had to change from the inside out.

CHAPTER ONE

YOUR MINDSET IS EVERYTHING

THE PRESSURE WAS overwhelming. As my employees saw their friends and family members succumb to job loss and foreclosures, they looked to me for reassurance that they would make it through the recession without losing their financial security. My CEO looked to me for ideas to bolster our revenue when most property owners were trying to keep their wallets closed. Tensions were even rising at home as my wife realized we could barely afford to provide for our two small children.

It felt like all my hard work had been for nothing... like the years I spent building a reputation and pursuing new opportunities only amounted to heartache and failure. I felt powerless and small. But what choice did I have? I had to find a way out.

As always, I turned to my strengths: ideas and innovation. But even as I searched for actionable solutions, I found myself dragged down by the feeling that this was all pointless. If I could never get my successes to stick, why even bother? Even if I could dig my way out of this hole, wouldn't I just end up back in it again?

I started following renowned business leaders and motivators, hoping they could give me some reason to hope, some reason to keep trying. This was when I heard the idea that would change my life.

> "Before you go and explore the world outside of you, explore the world inside of you."

The idea was that I had to confront the parts of myself that I had always avoided... my fears, my shortcomings, my self-sabotaging tendencies. The more I looked within, the more I realized there was a clear connection between my internal life and my external life. When my mind was open and engaged, everything seemed to go my way. When I felt fearful or cynical, communication stalled, all my ideas seemed stupid, and every problem looked like a steel wall blocking my path. These rules applied whether I was in the heart of a recession or at the height of my career.

In other words, it didn't matter what was happening *around* me. My success depended on what was happening *within* me.

I had to change my mindset. And so do you.

Admittedly, this is easier said than done. Having a positive mindset is not the same thing as positive thinking. It's not even quite the same as having a positive attitude. Your mindset is more than just the words you say to yourself and the smile you show to your team. Rather, a mindset is a personal belief system that determines how you approach opportunities and challenges... both emotionally and strategically.

Developing a new mindset takes time. When your first business is about to go bankrupt, you certainly can plaster on a smile and *tell* everybody that you see this challenge as an opportunity to explore a new direction... but you don't actually *feel* that way. Inside, you're filled with panic and self-doubt. That's not something you can change with a day of positive thinking.

This is the exact challenge we're going to confront over the course of this book. I am going to show you how to shift your perspective over time, so you can overcome current challenges and be better prepared with a positive outlook when the next obstacle rolls around. I'm not teaching you how to look on the bright side when things get tough. I'm teaching you how to transform your mindset *every day*, in good times and bad, so that positivity and growth are not an outfit you put on, but an integral part of who you are and the way you think about challenges.

This process takes hard work and genuine commitment. But it's worth it. When you change your mindset, you change your life.

Your Outer World Reflects Your Inner World

Have you ever had an argument with someone, dug your heels in, got a little ferocious, and then wound up embarrassed when you realized you completely misread the situation?

Maybe after a long, hard day at work, you mistook a spouse's innocent question about whether you'd paid the bills for an accusation that you're not pulling your weight. Or maybe after you spent the morning ruminating over falling sales numbers, an employee's request for vacation time feels like evidence that your staff is lazy and uninvested in the work.

It happens all the time. Without realizing it, we are constantly creating stories to explain our external circumstances. Because we're not aware of this habit, we mistake the stories we tell ourselves for actual reality.

Consider what goes on in your head when you wake up in the morning. You probably imagine the day ahead. If you're like most people, you gravitate towards the negative. You mentally prepare for the things you dread, like the pile of responsibilities waiting on your desk or a potentially confrontational meeting with an employee. By the time you get to work, you already feel worn-down and burned out. Your receptionist says you missed a call from a disgruntled customer and your immediate thought is, "Ugh, figures."

Now let's say you start the morning by imagining all the incredible things you are going to do with your day. You think about how good it will feel to get started on a new project. You think of this tricky conversation with your employee as an opportunity to make your life easier from here on out. By the time you get to work, you're inspired and energized. Your receptionist says you missed a call from a disgruntled customer and you immediately embrace this opportunity to prove your value to a buyer.

Nothing external changes between these two scenarios. The only change that occurs is within you. This is what I call the Mirror Concept... and it's key to not only understanding your greatest struggles as a business owner, but also understanding how to overcome those struggles.

The Mirror Concept

We paint everything with meaning. Everything.

To a gardener, a dandelion is a weed. To a botanist, it's an herb. To a child, it's a wildflower. The plant itself never changes. What changes is the person describing it.

This is the Mirror Concept. Your perception of an experience, object, place, or person is a direct reflection of your inner life. You may think you call a dandelion a weed because it is, in fact, a weed. But the truth is, you call it a weed because you have experiences and biases that cause you to see that plant as a nuisance... not as something beautiful or an important part of the ecosystem.

When you understand the Mirror Concept, you understand how your mindset can influence your professional success. If you want to run your business with a sense of clarity and purpose, you must cultivate those qualities within yourself. A chaotic mind will only see chaos. A fearful mind only sees danger.

But a creative mind sees possibility. A focused mind sees clear solutions.

Even the words you say out loud to yourself help shape your reality. When you talk about your goals, identify opportunities, and choose positive language over negative language, you begin to see possibilities instead of obstacles.

Of course, it isn't always that simple. Mindset isn't just about choosing positivity over negativity and clarity over chaos. We are complex human beings with complex histories, and those histories influence our perception.

I discovered this myself when I decided to finally confront my stutter. I had grown up with a speech impediment. And to the objective observer, that's all my stutter was: a speech impediment.

But to me, the stutter was an invisible wall between me and other people. I believed I'd never be able to fully express myself or share my ideas because my speech impediment would be too big a distraction for my listeners. When I established 911 Restoration, I declared myself "The Ideas Guy," closing myself up in my office and leaving it up to my CEO to communicate my ideas to the team. But then the 2008 Recession hit. I discovered that my company was floundering and I would have to take control of my own business by stepping in as CEO. This meant I'd have to get over my fear of speaking in front of a group.

To do this, I volunteered to speak to high school students about overcoming struggle to design a successful career.

The first time I stepped up to that podium, all I could see were bored faces, confused faces, and eyes uncomfortably shifting away when my stutter appeared. This was what I had seen in public speaking scenarios all my life. Even in small social get-togethers, I was always so sure that my speaking made everybody feel awkward or impatient.

The truth was, I felt awkward and impatient. The discomfort I saw in the crowd was actually my Mirror, reflecting my own insecurity back to me.

On some level, I understood this. So, I kept facing those kids, reminding myself time and again that the meaning I gave the situation was a meaning of my own invention. Sure enough, after one presentation, I overheard a student tell a teacher, "This was the most inspiring presentation we've had." From then on, my audience looked completely different to me. They were no longer disinterested teenagers shifting in their seats. They were young people with dreams and struggles similar to my own... kids in search of a connection and guidance.

Nothing changed except my mindset.

It's About Progress, Not Perfection

Here's the secret to cultivating the mindset of a successful business owner:

Focus on growth, not results.

The difference between you and the world's most successful entrepreneurs is not that they're so sure of their greatness. It's that they're sure of their ability to *become* great. You can try to psych yourself up for an important cold call by telling yourself over and over that you're the best at sales. But that technique isn't going to work if your track record says otherwise. You're still going to make the call feeling like a failure and a fraud.

But imagine if you told yourself, "I am capable of learning new sales skills. I can find creative ways to use my strengths to improve my sales pitch. I will practice, improve, and use this opportunity to get a little better at a skill that will help me grow my company over time."

This is the mindset we are building towards. It's not about unchecked self-celebration. It's about believing that you can handle any challenge because you are capable of change.

As you progress through this book, you will learn how to begin with small changes so you can train your mind to turn its focus toward growth and self-improvement. These small adjustments also help you cultivate a more positive attitude about yourself.

Let's say you decide your first small change will be to wake up fifteen minutes earlier every day so you can eat a healthy breakfast and arrive at work energized. This change is an investment in yourself. It's a *minor* investment, but you are still making a sacrifice (fifteen extra minutes of sleep) because deep down, you trust yourself to make that sacrifice worthwhile.

Now, you will stumble from time to time, even with the small changes. You may oversleep one morning or find yourself rushing out the door without breakfast to respond to an emergency at work. When this happens, just focus on getting back into your new routine the next day. Don't give yourself a hard time. Remember: you are trying to transform your mindset so your Mirror reflects positivity, not frustration and self-resentment. Set your focus on your potential, not on your mistakes.

As you continue on through your journey of growth, you will gradually make more and bigger changes. Each change is further evidence that you actually do believe in yourself... that you believe you are worth your own investment.

And if you are worth the investment, that must mean you have what it takes to create a thriving business.

✎ Exercise: Check Yourself in the Mirror

Transforming your mindset is a journey. The journey will be long. Sometimes you'll be struggling up steep mountain trails, other times you'll have an easy stroll over flat terrain. Either way, you should start by doing a little stretching to wake up those muscles.

Think of an obstacle standing between you and your business goals. Start with a small one. Maybe you keep losing money on marketing campaigns that fall flat. Maybe you're dreading a tough conversation about an employee's poor performance.

Take out a sheet of paper and write down how you currently plan to approach this problem. Look at your strategy, now written out in actual words. What does this plan tell you about what's going on inside you?

If you can't see evidence of your mindset, try looking at the issue a different way. How would you approach the exact same problem if you were focused on:

- How tired you are?
- How many other fires you have to put out?
- How much is at stake?
- Other life experiences that may have prepared you to handle this issue?
- What you hope to get out of this experience, challenge, or conversation?
- How this obstacle can help you develop a new strength?

The more you open your mind to other approaches, the more aware you are of the fact that your current plan is not actually the only option or even the most rational option. Your approach is only *one* alternative, inspired by your subjective view of the situation.

You always have more options than you think. It's true that you can't always control which challenges arise in your work. But how you approach those challenges is entirely up to you.

CHAPTER TWO

WHY YOUR MINDSET IS WHAT IT IS

WHAT WOULD IT take for me to convince you that polar bears live in Texas?

It would probably take a lot, right? You have an entire life-time of experiences telling you that polar bears live in the Arctic. Your science teacher told you so. You've seen the polar bear lifestyle portrayed in cartoons, commercials, and nature documentaries. Polar bears even serve as mascots for ice and snow cones. Even if I could deliver a passionate speech that made you *want* to believe polar bears live in Texas, it still wouldn't be enough to change your ingrained sense of reality.

And that is why changing your mindset is a long process.

We tend to talk about "mindset" like it's an attitude or a point of view. But it's just not that simple. Your mindset is an organized belief system. It's a perceived "reality" built from decades of personal experience. Unlike your knowledge of polar bear habitats, your mindset is faulty. But that doesn't matter. To you, it feels just as certain.

So how do you change a lifetime of deeply-held beliefs?

You start by understanding where those beliefs come from. If I were really on a mission to convince you polar bears come from El Paso, I'd have to explain how your teacher could be so wrong and why television misled you.

That is what we are working on in this chapter. We are going to take a good, hard look at everything you believe about yourself, your circumstances, and the universe. I'm going to show you how to work backwards so you can understand the origins of your belief system. Ultimately, you're going to learn that you have been making a lot of decisions based on misinformation and outright lies. When you understand this, you can begin to let go of the faulty mindset that has been holding you back.

Let's start with the big issue: the way you see yourself.

The Problem of Self-Confidence

This is one of the great challenges of entrepreneurship. We know self-confidence is necessary for success, but we also come face-to-face with our own shortcomings every single day. As a business owner, you constantly confront failure, your own miscalculations, the doubts of others, and personal weaknesses. When things are going well, you feel great about yourself. Your mind is open and alert and exploding with new ideas. When things are going poorly, you shut down. You don't truly believe you have what it takes to overcome and succeed, so... you *don't* overcome and succeed.

The problem is that you are using the wrong yardstick to measure your self-worth.

A lot of people use symbols of success to gauge their own value... things like nice cars, a big house, or an attractive spouse. Entrepreneurs are especially prone to this habit, because we spend all day thinking up strategies to earn more, grow more, and achieve more. We size up the competition by noting how big their storefront is or what part of town they live in. If our friends and family are impressed with us, they're impressed because they see that we doubled our staff or took an expensive vacation. The world celebrates us for our external accomplishments, and those accomplishments become our own gauge for self-satisfaction.

The truth is, you are not what you own.

You are not what you have accomplished.

You are so much bigger than your car, your house, and your lead close rates.

Sometimes your successes are hard-earned and sometimes things just sort of fall into place. Sometimes failure happens *to* you and sometimes you're the cause. None of it says anything about your personal value.

Now, this is where many entrepreneurs say, "Wait—if I succeed because I worked hard or fail because I messed up, doesn't that success or failure indicate my value as a business owner? It's a direct result of my efforts. It's proof of what I am (or am not) capable of."

This is the exact mindset we are trying to break free from.

Let's say you have a difficult time making decisions. You are an analytical person, and every important move you make in your business takes longer than it should because you tend to over-examine your options. You obsess over the perfect wording for every PPC ad. You lose an entire hour of your day crafting and workshopping a Pulitzer-worthy response to one negative online review. Your under-staffed office struggles to keep the business running smoothly while you analyze resumes and compare interview answers.

You get the idea.

Now, most business owners would look at their hyper-analytical habits and say, "I'm too obsessive and that's why I'm failing." You can see how this mindset is loaded with negative views of self worth. *I'm too obsessive. I'm a failure.*

On the other hand, a business owner who sees his career through a growth mindset says, "I have an analytical mind. I am going to learn how to use that skill to improve my business—like when I look for weaknesses in an ineffective marketing strategy. I am also going to learn techniques for quieting my obsessive mind when it prevents me from moving forward."

Now, what is the biggest difference between these two statements?

The first statement suggests that you are hyper-analytical. That is your defining quality.

The second statement acknowledges your analytical tendencies, but it doesn't define you as obsessive. Instead, the second statement defines you as *changeable*.

This detail—the way you define who you are—is what separates those who struggle from those who excel.

Who are You *Really*?

You are limitless. You are completely capable of becoming the person you want to be. You have every reason to believe your dreams are possible, because you have all the skills you need to make those dreams come true.

This is not an empty attempt to boost your self-esteem. I'm just telling you the facts. You are capable of excellence *because you are capable of change*. That's all you need—the ability to learn and evolve.

We have a tendency to carve our identities in stone, never questioning our self-imposed limits. And yet, everything around us changes. A tiny seed becomes an oak tree. Leaves curl up, die, fall, and are crushed into dust. Rocks shift with the current of the riverbed and grow smoother over time. Caterpillars disappear inside a cocoon, liquify, and somehow emerge as a butterfly.

Transformation is natural and necessary, and only human beings resist it. That's such a tremendous loss because we are also the only creatures who have an imagination. We can dream up new solutions and expand our own opportunities. Don't ever tell yourself you're "only human." Your humanity is the most powerful thing about you.

My point being, you are not your car, your house, or even your resume. The one quality that will truly define you throughout your entire life is your changeability.

Exercise: "I am Not"

If you hope to create a new mindset, you have to let go of the old mindset. In the context of self-confidence, this means you must release the old standards you've been using to measure your worth.

I recommend creating a nightly routine of mentally listing all the things you are *not*. As you lie in bed, before you fall asleep, think through all the traits you have leaned on to justify both self-doubt and self-confidence. Tell yourself:

> *"I am not my car."*
> *"I am not my house."*
> *"I am not my bank account."*
> *"I am not my sales ability."*
> *"I am not my organizational skills."*
> *"I am not my neighbor's envy."*

Do this every night. It seems like such a small effort, and that's the beauty of it. This routine is easy to maintain, but its long-term effects are powerful. Little by little, you retrain your brain, mentally disconnecting from standards of self-worth that do not define you.

You become more open to seeing yourself for the creative, changeable force that you are.

The Problem of Emotional DNA

Now let's widen our lens beyond self-confidence and take a look at the way you see the larger world.

We like to fantasize that we are independent thinkers, never influenced by outside forces. Unfortunately, that isn't even remotely true. Your beliefs come from many places. You are shaped by your socio-economic class, your religious community, your educational background, your friendships, your hardships, and about a million other factors. As you go through your process of growth, you will begin to see evidence of all these influences. For now, let's focus on the first and greatest influence on your belief system: your parents... and even your grandparents.

You inherit your parents' and ancestors' emotional DNA the same way you inherit their eyes, smile, and laugh.

This is true both in a genetic sense and in a behavioral sense. Research in the last several years suggests that traumatic experiences can actually trigger epigenetic changes that can be passed on to the next generation. As for the behavioral end of things, your parents' beliefs, opinions, and choices are inspired by their own life experiences. And because your parents are your first and greatest influence, their belief system inevitably becomes *your* belief system.

Let's say your mother sees road trips as dangerous and nerve-wracking because she was in a harrowing car accident as a child. You then adopt this same perspective, having spent an entire childhood triple-checking your seatbelt and avoiding freeways to put her mind at ease.

Now, what if you have actively tried *not* to follow in your parents' footsteps?

These ideas apply to you, too. By choosing to do the opposite of what your parents would do, you're still living by a belief system that is a direct reaction to your parents' belief system.

So, what does all this psychoanalysis have to do with your career as a business owner or aspiring business owner?

More than you might expect.

If you grew up with parents who saw wealthy people as greedy and self-interested, you probably have an internal, unexamined limit for how successful *you* can be without becoming a horrible human being. If your parents were immigrants who were eager to help you blend in, you might experience anxiety when it's time to take bold steps in order to stand out in your market. If you had an unstable childhood because your parents were reckless with money, you might have trouble investing in new carpet extractors as long as your older, clunkier models still work.

The point here is not to blame your parents for problems in your business. The point is to become more aware of why you see the world the way you do. One of my great epiphanies came when I realized I was embarrassed to show my parents my home in California. When I moved to the U.S. with big dreams, I fantasized about building an impressive life that would make my parents proud. But when I actually made that dream come true, I felt awkward and a little guilty. I grew up in a home where money was scarce... a source of tension and struggle. Now, to have this big, comfortable home... it felt extravagant, rude, and careless.

So, what does that have to do with my choices as a business owner?

In 2008, I lost loads of money in real estate investments and discovered that 911 Restoration was barely hanging on. I re-evaluated my business decisions and realized that I'd been spreading myself too thin, chasing too many partnerships and investment opportunities instead of throwing myself whole-heartedly into the company I was passionate about.

"But I have to do that," I thought. *"If there's a good opportunity to make money, I have to seize it."*

But clearly that wasn't true. By pursuing *every* opportunity, I wasn't giving *any* opportunity the focus it deserved. And when I examined that choice honestly through the lens of my life experience, I realized that my business strategies did not come from entrepreneurial insight. They came from ingrained ideas about money.

Money is scarce. You have to scrape together whatever resources you can. Don't expect to build wealth. You were not meant to be a wealthy person.

In other words, I was sabotaging myself. I was not *actively* pursuing the type of career I wanted—a career defined by purpose and financial abundance. Instead, I was *reacting* to the beliefs and fears I'd inherited from my parents.

Reaction Versus Action

Business owners who have a positive growth mindset are always focused on creation. Struggling entrepreneurs are not. They are locked in a victim mentality, which means they are constantly in reaction mode.

Here are a few scenarios to illustrate the difference:

Two business owners wake up groggy.

The creative business owner is focused on his plans for the day, so he gets up, drinks a glass of water to rehydrate, and does some stretching and light exercise to get energized for the day ahead.

The reactive business owner is focused on the feeling of sleepiness, so he hits snooze, drags himself out of bed twenty minutes later, and grabs a sugary breakfast bar on the way out the door.

Two business owners have a problem with a burned-out employee.

The creative business owner eagerly plans a meeting with this employee, imagining how she can use this opportunity to find ways to help her team find more fulfillment in their work.

The reactive business owner dreads the confrontation and puts off saying anything in the hopes that the employee will find his way out of his funk.

Two business owners sit down to spend two hours working on a new project that could double revenue for their business. As soon as they sit down, an angry customer calls with a complaint.

The creative business owner isn't affected by the call. He has told the receptionist that he is not to be disturbed for the next two hours, and he has worked hard to mentor a manager who he fully trusts to handle conflicts like this one. He can focus on creating without worrying about what he's missing.

The reactive business owner takes the call and spends the next forty-five minutes solving the customer's problem.

If you are like most struggling business owners, you are not making active, creative decisions. You are simply reacting to the panicked demands of your emotional DNA. When a conflict arises, instead of asking, "What can I create from this moment?" you ask, "How can I avoid failure, embarrassment, or pain?"

If you want to grow your business, you have to give up your reactive mindset. And the first step is to understand what it is you are reacting to.

Exercise: Emotional DNA Inventory

Take out a sheet of paper. At the top, write down an obstacle you are facing right now. It doesn't have to be a big one; it can be a meeting you're dreading or a project you're stuck on.

Write down how you have been planning to approach this challenge.

Then, think of five different people who have had a major influence on your life, especially in your childhood. Parents and siblings are a great place to start.

Write down how each of these people would approach your obstacle.

Now, look for patterns. Do you see your approach reflected in anyone else's? Look for choices that are the same as yours *and* choices that are the polar opposite.

When you notice a parallel (or opposite) approach, ask yourself, "Why would this person handle this issue in this way? What influences have made them feel like this was the best course of action?"

One powerful result of this exercise is that you discover how little your decisions are influenced by the actual moment in front of you. Often, they are based on emotions you inherited and experiences that are completely unrelated to the obstacle you're confronting.

And once you see it, you can't unsee it.

The Problem of Your Own Lies

The third element contributing to your faulty mindset is your own deceitful mind.

You lie to yourself all the time. These lies are the stories you create to explain the world around you and who you are within it.

To be fair, you're not *aware* that you're lying. In most cases, you're not even aware that you've made up any kind of story in the first place. That's because we don't call it storytelling. We call it "logic."

Your mind has one concern: keeping you safe. Consider your earliest memory of injury. It only took one mistake to understand that fire is hot, bees sting, and falling out of a tree hurts. Your mind turned that lesson into a neon warning sign, ready to flash bright red at the sound of buzzing or the sensation of heat.

In cases such as these, your mind's desperate need to protect you is helpful and practical. The problem is that your mind does the same thing with *every* negative experience, no matter how abstract or complicated.

Consider my belief system surrounding money. Because I grew up in a poor home, my mind prepared me for a lifetime of financial struggle. It's no wonder that I spent so many years spread thin, working long hours to follow through on multiple commitments that ultimately earned significantly less than what I earn now. I didn't think I could earn money any other way, and deep down, I didn't even believe I deserved to prosper.

The mind is so focused on self-preservation that it doesn't bother to differentiate between fact and theory. It just tells you you're in debt because you're not good with money. Your date didn't go well because all the good ones are taken. Your sales are down because you don't have what it takes to run a business. The mind insists that all these explanations are as logical and scientifically sound as "Fire is hot," and just as with "Fire is hot," the moral of the story is "Stay away." Don't try to build wealth. Don't bother getting your hopes up about finding love. Don't try to save your business; you'll only make it worse.

You have to stop buying your own lies.

⬙ Exercise: Let Go of the Past

If you could change one thing about yourself as a business owner, what would it be? Your poor sales skills? Your tech incompetence? Your fear of even starting a business in the first place?

Whatever it is, take a moment to consider why you think that shortcoming is not something you can overcome. What evidence do you have to support that belief?

You may be surprised by how quickly the memories surface. Do you keep putting off that pitch to a high-value client because you failed speech and debate in high school? Are you refusing to update your office's technology because you feel old and obsolete when your kid helps you with computer problems at home? Is your dream of becoming a business owner still just a dream because you know how it feels to fail massively and publicly?

Our minds are deeply entrenched in old wounds, even when we're not aware of it. This holds us back, because our energy follows our focus. If you're fixated on old memories of awkward networking events, you will only become a worse networker. On the other hand, if you focus on your potential to grow and thrive, guess what happens?

Exactly. You grow and thrive.

Take a moment right now to think about one thing you would love to try... something you consider beyond your capabilities. It can be something small. Maybe you want to explore social media marketing for your business or you'd like to speak at the next Chamber of Commerce event. Ask yourself three questions:

1. **What will happen if I attempt this change and it goes well?** What could it mean for your career, your company, or your self-confidence?

2. **What will happen if I never try to take this step forward?**

3. **Realistically, what will happen if I fail?** What do you actually have to lose? The risks are almost always much lower than we believe them to be.

If these questions aren't enough to inspire you to make the change, try a reverse exercise. Look ten to twenty years into your past. What one change do you wish you made ages ago?

Take a moment to feel that wistfulness… that sense of regret and disappointment. Then, commit to eliminating that kind of regret for your Future Self.

Finally, if you really struggle to shake the memory of past failures, take a deep breath and remind yourself:

- What year it is
- How old you are
- How much time has passed since that memory
- That you are a different person
- That you are limitless and capable of change

Try doing this exercise whenever you face a challenge and feel that tug of self-doubt. Remember that by giving into that doubt, you are effectively living the past, and the past has nothing to do with your future.

- Einstein's past was full of teachers who considered him "lazy" and "distracted."
- Abraham Lincoln's past included eight lost elections.
- Surfer Bethany Hamilton had a shark attack in her past when she won the Explorer Women's Division of the NSSSA National Championship.

Do you see how much you can accomplish when you choose to stop living in the past and charge boldly into the future?

CHAPTER THREE

THE JOURNEY FROM VICTIM TO CREATOR

SO, WHAT NOW? You know mindset is important. You know your current mindset isn't helping you. And you know changing your mindset will take time and effort.

But what kind of effort? And where do you start?

First, let's clarify goals. As we move through this process, I encourage you to focus on one, single objective.

Growth.

Now, as a business owner, you have other goals. Concrete goals. You want to bring in more leads, double your revenue, or open three more locations. These measurable objectives are important for tracking the success of your business strategies. Clearly defined goals also help you unify your team around a shared mission.

But in order to reach your concrete objectives, you have to first focus on your own growth as a leader. If you are stuck in old habits, so is your team. If you can't access a positive attitude, your staff won't be able to, either. And if you're not thinking in terms of personal improvement and professional innovation, guess what. The people you lead will also operate in maintenance mode.

On the other hand, when you focus on transforming your mindset and growing as a human being, you get better, lasting results. You don't just push your team to achieve a single goal, you inspire them to be creative and forward-thinking, so they proactively pursue bigger and bigger goals long into the future. Meanwhile, *you* find a new sense of purpose and fulfillment in your work because it's not just about raking in cash; it's about waking up each morning excited to expand your dream and stretch your capabilities.

Now, as entrepreneurs, we like to measure and benchmark everything. So, how do we do that for something as complex as an inner growth journey?

I've got you covered.

The Four Stages of Growth

The ultimate goal is to get to a place where you know beyond a shadow of a doubt that you can handle whatever obstacle comes your way. That state of mind is the entrepreneurial mindset we're talking about. "I can handle this, because I can change and create. I control my future."

Reaching that level of certainty takes time. You will not be there by the time you finish reading this book. The only way to truly convince yourself that you can adapt and thrive is by actually adapting and thriving. It's going to take a while to override that lifetime of negative experiences and limiting beliefs.

Throughout the process, you will always be in one of four stages. I recommend checking in with yourself from time to time to see where you are. Think of it like sales numbers or employee satisfaction surveys. If you want to see change, you need to track progress.

STAGE 1: VICTIM

The Mindset: You see yourself as powerless. Everything just happens to you. You have no control and no choices. Even if you accept the blame for your problems, you do not believe you are capable of improving the situation. You are who you are, and you can't be any different. You're stuck because your staff is incompetent or your spouse is unsupportive or you are not talented enough.

Your more successful friend is either lucky or inherently better than you.

STAGE 2: HOPEFUL

The Mindset: You are ready to entertain the possibility that you have more control over your future than you thought you did. You made a few small attempts to improve your situation and a couple of them worked. You have also started paying closer attention to the way your successful friend runs his business. He tells you how hard it was to fire a problematic employee even though he knew the company would be better for it. It occurs to you that he might be on his own journey of growth.

Part of you still wonders if business success is mostly a matter of luck and connections, but you feel a new glimmer of hope anyway. Maybe you really can create the life you want.

STAGE 3: BELIEVER

Mindset: You have now overcome enough challenges to know it *is* possible. You have confronted obstacles you once thought were beyond your capabilities, and you now see that you are a stronger, wiser person because you struggled and were forced to grow. Lately, you feel genuine gratitude for the challenges life gives you.

It may still be difficult to approach growth opportunities with a sense of excitement and positivity, but you do truly believe that you can always summon the strength you need. You may not yet be fully aware of your true abilities, but you do understand that you have the ability to make your own life better.

STAGE 4: CREATOR

The Mindset: You are the architect of your life. You know this for a fact.

Every obstacle is a gift. You approach new challenges with a sense of curiosity and excitement, because you know each struggle helps you transform into a better, stronger, more capable version of yourself. You live actively instead of reactively. You are driven by creativity, not fear.

In this stage, you become a mentor to others. You inspire and empower your team to focus on growth and progress over fear and self-judgment. Most likely, success comes more easily now. But you no longer depend on success for happiness and a sense of self-worth. The mission of ongoing self-improvement provides fulfillment in good times and bad.

Where Do You Stand?

In the following chapters, I'll walk you through all the practical steps you can take to start cultivating a mindset of confidence and creation. But before we jump in, take a moment to gauge where you are right now.

Are you:

- A **Victim** who sees himself or herself as powerless in an unpredictable world?
- A **Hopeful** who is willing to entertain the idea that personal transformation is possible?
- A **Believer** who knows he or she can overcome challenges when it's necessary?
- A **Creator** who eagerly treats every situation as an opportunity to build a better life and career?

Once you determine your current stage of growth, pull out your physical or digital calendar and find the date that's exactly six months from today. Record your current stage of growth on that date.

When that date rolls around, refer back to this list. Are you still a Victim, or have you become a Hopeful?

Our mindset evolves so gradually, we often don't even realize anything has changed. It's important to check in every now and then... to look back after some time has passed and recognize that you are, in fact, making major strides forward.

I also recommend checking in with yourself on a weekly basis. While you can't change your entire mindset over the course of a single week, you should find yourself testing a new, Hopeful mindset every now and then.

Take a moment every weekend to look back on the previous week and ask yourself:

- What situation did I handle like a Victim this week?
- What situation did I handle like a Hopeful?
- Did I ever act like a Believer or a Creator?

Also think ahead to the week that lies before you. What new challenge is approaching? How would you handle it:

- As a Victim?
- As a Hopeful?
- As a Believer?
- As a Creator?

Then, once you've worked out the difference, commit to handling that situation with the Creator's solution. When you follow through on that commitment, take a moment to notice and celebrate that success. You might even want to keep a record of all the times you acted as a Hopeful, Believer, or Creator. After all, collecting evidence of growth makes it easier to believe in the process. And believing in the process is how you pass through each stage from Victim to Creator.

So... ready to dive in?

CHAPTER FOUR

FIND CLARITY

NOW THAT YOU know how to identify those beliefs that hold you back, it's time to learn how to focus on the ideas that propel you forward.

In order to do that, you have to know what you want. I'm not talking about the material results you want, like higher revenue, a second location, or a vacation home. I'm talking about the big questions, like:

- What kind of impact do you want to make on the world?
- What aspects of your life today will matter the most to you when you are eighty years old?
- Who do you want to become as a person and as a leader?

- What kind of legacy do you hope to build?
- How do you want your employees and customers to feel when they work with you?
- What is your greater purpose?

When you can answer those questions, you become more aware of what matters. This helps you make better, more effective decisions on a day-to-day basis.

Let me explain.

Making the Most of Your Remarkable Mind

You know your mind is a powerful force. Just think of everything we've discussed over the last three chapters. Your mind has already proven its vast creative capabilities, weaving complex systems of "logic" designed to protect you both physically and emotionally. If it can do all that *without* your deliberate involvement, imagine how powerful your mind can be when you use it with intention.

I'll use myself as an example. As you have probably figured out by now, I believe challenges exist to help us become better people and build towards a better life. I have found fulfillment by centering my life around this philosophy, and I consider it my purpose to empower others with this idea. This purpose guides me in writing books like this and leading my franchisees to success. It also guides my decision-making as CEO of 911 Restoration.

- When conflicts or mistakes occur within the company, **I encourage all team members to treat the issue as an opportunity for growth.**
- When designing the voice and brand of 911 Restoration, **I focused on the messaging that meant the most to me:** 911 Restoration is here to give property owners a Fresh Start after disaster.
- **I actively motivate all franchisees to promote a growth mindset within their own teams.** This helps their staff discover a sense of fulfillment in their work, which leads to great attitudes on the job, which enhances the customer experience.
- Even in the midst of a pandemic, when it was so easy to feel overwhelmed by the inevitability of another recession, **I held my focus on that same question.** *"How can I use this challenge to create new opportunities for myself and others?"* I added property sanitization to our list of services, offering home and business owners peace of mind at a time when keeping up with CDC disinfection guidelines felt impossible.

You have an incredible ability to problem solve and innovate. But you can only tap into that talent when you have clarity. If you try to draw up a marketing plan and you don't know what you want other than "more money," you're going to overwhelm your mind with meaningless options and make decisions from a place of fear.

You see that your competitors are advertising on Facebook, so you do, too. Another competitor uses humor in their ads, so you do, too. You go to a seminar and learn that you need a blog to drive traffic to your website, so you frantically throw a blog together.

In other words, you blindly do what you think you have to do to keep up. You don't forge your own path through active efforts such as:

- Analyzing customer needs to design value-added services
- Looking for opportunities to enhance services or productivity through innovation
- Promoting professional excellence for yourself and your team
- Cultivating long-term thinking instead of obsessing over short-term obstacles

These are things you *should* be focused on. But do that, you need clarity.

Exercise: Find Space in Your Mind

It should be easy to say what we want. And yet, our truest desires are often buried under a long list of "should wants" and "nice to haves." It becomes very difficult to hear your inner voice—the voice telling you what really matters to you.

If you have trouble finding the answers to the questions I posed at the beginning of this chapter, that's okay. It takes time to achieve clarity. Even when you know exactly what you want, you still have to fight off constant distractions and lingering self-doubt. So be patient, and take this day by day.

I recommend you start seeking clarity by identifying one simple activity that helps you create space in the mind. That's a fancy way of asking, "When are you actually able to disconnect from the chaos and hear yourself think?"

Is it during your morning jog? While you're engaging in a relaxing hobby like cooking or fishing? Have you tried meditation?

Think about how you feel in that moment and find a way to make that feeling part of your daily routine. Consider something like:

- Taking a walk in the park on your lunch break
- Stretching in your backyard every morning
- Starting a meditation practice
- Taking fifteen minutes every day to mindfully engage in a hobby
- Scheduling non-negotiable exercise time every day

Whatever method works for you, start small. You are going to hear me say that a lot in this book. When you start with a small, sustainable goal, you set yourself up for inevitable success. That success boosts your self-trust, which makes it easier to make big changes later on. Having said that, I want to note that even the small steps must be made with big determination. Move forward with passion, remembering that every change—no matter how minor—ultimately launches you into a life of success and fulfillment.

You will also begin to notice that even these small moments of clarity can have a major effect on your overall mindset, as long as you maintain a consistent routine. Little by little, you find yourself becoming more conscious of the chaos in your head and better able to separate the lies of your worried mind from the truth of the situation in front of you.

Once you do that, you're well on your way to becoming unstoppable.

Equip Yourself for a Long Journey

The ultimate formula for professional success is clarity + energy. If you know exactly what you want *and* you have the energy to pursue it fully, there is nothing you cannot do.

In the coming chapters, I'll have more guidance for boosting your physical and mental energy. For now, let's talk about emotional energy.

I have warned you several times that changing your mindset is a long and difficult process. This includes any effort to find clarity. Most of the time, you'll be taking baby steps forward. Moving at this pace, it can be easy to feel like you're not making any progress at all. This makes it easy to feel burned out. You start to get the sense that none of this works and you should give up.

To avoid this feeling, make sure you see and celebrate all the small strides you're making. Notice when:

- You caught yourself thinking like a Victim and made the deliberate decision to handle a difficult situation like a Creator instead.
- You followed through on your commitment to spend a little time stretching every morning.
- You finally agreed to purchase the cutting-edge client management software your office manager has been pushing for, and you even scheduled time to focus on learning the system in the coming week.
- You put a block on all your social media applications during work hours—one less distraction so you can focus on what matters.

These may be small successes, but they're successes nonetheless. And if you take the time to notice them, you will also notice how these little victories become bigger, more frequent victories.

Nothing propels you forward like the thrill of a win. So never let a win go unnoticed.

CHAPTER FIVE

DECIDE WHO WILL BE YOUR GUIDE

ONCE YOU KNOW where you're headed, you need to find someone who can help you get there.

Finding a mentor is another non-negotiable step in your journey of growth. You cannot skip this step by just reading more books or following entrepreneurial thought leaders on social media.

Why?

Because a mentor is more than a source of advice. The right mentor pushes you to keep going when you feel like giving up. They help you identify personal weaknesses and find opportunities to build on your strengths. They don't let you get away with excuses or allow you to blame others for your own shortcomings. They point out flaws in your approach and hold you accountable when you fail to follow through on commitments.

In other words, the right mentor is not afraid to tell you when you're being stupid, short-sighted, or self-destructive.

This is especially important because it will be harder to find these qualities in your employees and peers as you discover more success. The more you grow your business, the less inclined others are to criticize you. Now, there are many reasons for this phenomenon. Those who have achieved less than you might not have the confidence to question your methods. Those who work with you may want to keep you happy, believing that you hold their fate in your hands. And many people may simply default to the logic that you have found such success because you're always right.

Whatever the reason, this constant positive feedback can be a killer for your growth. I *do* believe that business owners need a little affirmation now and then. As you know, I also believe it's important to celebrate your successes. But when all you ever hear is that you're brilliant and innovative, you are going to stop evolving. There's no reason to change. Everyone around you says you're perfect.

A mentor does not operate this way. Their job is to challenge you, not to flatter you. They ensure your growth, not just today, but long into the future.

So, how do you connect with a mentor? And how do you find the best person to guide you on your journey?

Start by taking a closer look at your needs.

The Qualities of a Good Mentor

It's not enough to just find someone who has made a lot of money and start following their advice. Just like you, every successful entrepreneur has a unique set of values and principles. They are driven by their own sense of purpose.

When you're looking for a mentor, prioritize professionals whose values align with your own.

This is not to say that your mentor has to be exactly like you, but it's worth it to look for those similarities that inform the type of direction or insight you can expect from this person.

Start by identifying high performers in your field. If you own a plumbing company, you don't have to find another plumber, but it is a good idea to find another professional in the home services or construction field. Then, do some research.

This might include:

- Finding articles by or about them online
- Following them on social media
- Attending events where they are featured as a speaker
- Reaching out to acquaintances who have worked for or with them

Try to find out more about their journey to success and the philosophies that guide them. Do what you can to answer questions such as:

- What challenges did this person face on their way up? Would they be able to understand my struggle?
- What type of company culture have they cultivated? Does this reflect the type of business I want to build for myself?
- How do others talk about them? Do they have the kind of reputation I hope to earn?
- Are they still growing and transforming? (You're looking for a "yes" to this question.)

Use these answers to narrow down your list of possible mentors to those whose careers aligns with the vision you have for your own professional life. Then, find an opportunity to connect with each individual and get to know them better. If you know them personally, this should be easy. But even if you've mostly admired them from afar, don't hesitate to invite them out for coffee or ask if you can pick their brain over video chat. (More on this in a moment.) Use these encounters to learn how your personalities gel.

- Do they explain concepts clearly?
- Do they understand your values and priorities?
- Do they understand your roadblocks?
- Does it seem like they can pick up on your strengths, weaknesses, and opportunities for self-improvement?
- Do they demonstrate respect for your career and genuine interest in your growth?
- Are they willing to be honest with you, or does it seem like they're dancing around your feelings?

Now, it's important to note that finding the right mentor is typically not a two-step process. You don't just make a list, meet everyone once, and narrow down your candidates. Often, a mentor/mentee relationship develops naturally as you get to know a professional you admire. With each interaction, you become more trusting of their advice, and they become more personally invested in your success. So please note that the checklists above are not designed to help you find the right mentor by next Tuesday. Rather, it's a framework to help you narrow your focus. Many entrepreneurs have wasted countless hours seeking advice from an incompatible mentor who just happened to have two vacation homes.

Remember: it's not about the *things* you want. It's about the career you want.

Finally, you should also consider your mentor's strengths. Work with someone who can offer guidance in areas where you typically feel a little lost. In fact, I recommend having several mentors, each with a different category of expertise. Look for a mentor in areas like:

- Entrepreneurship
- Finances
- Personal growth
- Marketing
- Organization
- Team management
- Home services
- Etc.

Nurturing these relationships takes time. But someday you'll have an expert to call in any situation, and you'll be grateful you put in the effort.

How to Find a Mentor

Entrepreneurs who have MBAs often have no trouble finding mentors. Mentorship is built into the educational system. Students graduate with a wide network of experts who know experts who know experts, and finding help feels natural and easy.

For those of us who came up as tradesmen, it's a different story. You may have had a mentor if you were lucky... possibly a good boss who nurtured your talent or a colleague who took you under their wing when you were starting out. But the idea of reaching out and directly asking for long-term guidance from a busy, successful professional probably feels a little unnatural. Even uncomfortable.

First, I want to assure you that every self-made entrepreneur has had several mentors. They know you need guidance as much as they did. If you reach out for advice, the worst that will happen is that the entrepreneur in question will be too busy. They will respect you for asking, and they will recognize that by reaching out, you prove you are proactive and worthy of someone's time and attention.

Second, I want you to understand that finding a mentor does not mean you have to ask someone to invest time and energy in your development just out of the goodness of their heart. Many professionals hold back from seeking mentorship because it sounds like a huge ask. But the truth is, there are basically two types of mentors you should be looking for:

- A professional who can occasionally provide advice in their area of expertise
- A major player in your field who serves as a member of your paid advisory board

Let's talk about the difference and how you can connect with both types of mentor.

Your Unpaid Mentor

This person is someone whose skills in a specific area exceed your own. They could be a whiz at finances, marketing, management, anything. This individual might be someone who is further along in their career than you are, but they don't have to be. They can be your peer. They just have to be able to give you great advice within their realm of expertise.

Your relationship with an unpaid mentor develops organically over time. Generally speaking, you don't ask them for loads of time or attention. They may or may not pay close attention to your career. In many cases, they don't reach out to offer unsolicited advice. But they are there for you when you need insight on a specific issue.

So how do you find this person and nurture the relationship?

Start by looking at your existing network. Is there anyone in that network who can help you in those areas where you need guidance? If the answer is no, it's time to expand your network. Attend industry events, check out seminars, and find opportunities to connect with other professionals.

If (or when) there is someone in your existing network that you'd like to learn from, take small steps to nurture that connection. You don't have to ask that person outright to be your mentor. In fact, you probably shouldn't. But do create opportunities to strengthen your connection. Try:

- Sending an email to congratulate them on a recent success.
- Asking them for advice on a small matter.
- Asking them for advice on a larger matter in exchange for coffee. Be sure to explain why you're interested in speaking to them specifically.
- Offering help. I have a two-way relationship with a few of my mentors. Because our strengths are different and we are similarly successful, each of us is able to offer advice, resources, and connections to help the other.

As the relationship progresses, remember to maintain regular communication. You don't have to get lunch once a month, but do reach out every now and then, even when you *don't* need advice. When you establish this type of friendly connection, the other person is almost always delighted to give you the help you ask for.

Now, let's take a look at a more structured form of mentorship.

Your Advisory Board

As my list of mentors expanded, I began to see what a powerful asset it was to have that kind of expertise on hand. I could reach out to these people with a challenging situation, and they'd give me the exact advice I needed to overcome the hurdle and advance my company. They got to know my career and goals, and they were more than happy to call me out for bad ideas or self-sabotaging behavior. I knew these colleagues played an essential role in my personal and professional growth. And that got me wondering: how much more could I grow if I had a structured mentor relationship?

What if, instead of reaching out casually on an as-needed basis, I were to schedule regular quarterly meetings with an expert? What if I knew I could count on this person for consistent follow-ups and even had them sign an NDA so I could speak with them openly about any aspect of my business? What if I could connect with a professional who saw mentorship as a responsibility, not just a favor... someone who would invest real time into fully understanding my vision, my strengths, and my team?

I knew I could never ask for this level of commitment for free. But by this point, I had every reason to believe that this kind of support was worth paying for, as long as I selected the right mentors.

I connected with two people who had both built highly successful franchise companies. Their successes aligned with my goals, which mean that they knew how to get where I was going. One of them had exceptional management skills—an area that has never been my strength. And both had respect for my team and a willingness to deliver hard truths if it meant helping me succeed. I asked them to be my two-man advisory board. For an annual fee, they would meet with me and my executive team every quarter.

This turned out to be one of the greatest investments I have ever made. Under their guidance, my team and I were able to reach new heights in record time.

I am going to tell you right now: you *need* an advisory board.

A lot of business owners think they should hold off on paying for mentorship until they have a larger company and a bigger budget. This is a mistake. The sooner you create a strong advisory board, the faster you advance your company. The cost of this mentorship is absolutely nothing compared to what you gain in business growth.

You should also be aware that you will never outgrow an advisory board. I still meet with mine every three months.

Now, how do you find the right advisory board?

Once again, you start by looking at your goals and areas of weakness. Because you're about to invest money in this person or people, you want to make sure you select a mentor who:

- Aligns with your vision and values
- Excels in at least one or two areas where you struggle
- Has (and will continue to have) more experience than you
- Has already achieved goals similar to your own

Now, you may already have someone like this in your existing support system. If not, it's time to get a little proactive.

Expand your network. Get to know the major players in your industry. Actively seek out those experts who will force you to grow, and when you've found a great match, bite the bullet and invest in your future.

The Mentee Mindset

Having a mentor is not always fun. Hopefully, this person encourages you, inspires you, and cheers you on. But—hopefully—they also present you with some hard truths. You need a mentor because you have blind spots. We all do. Even as you build towards that Creator mindset, there will still be shortcomings in your attitude and approach that you are unable to recognize on your own.

Your mentor forces you to see these flaws. And it is almost always annoying. Sometimes even infuriating if you're not in the right headspace.

Before every encounter with your mentor—whether you're sending an email asking for advice or casually meeting for lunch—take a moment to remind yourself:

- You need insight, not flattery.
- Constructive criticism is a gift, not an insult.
- Your goal is growth, not perfection.

Be open to hearing your mentor and let your ego take a backseat to your growth.

Having said that, you can be critical of your mentor's feedback. Sometimes a mentorship turns out to be a bad match. It's okay to realize that you don't trust your mentor's guidance. You should never follow anyone blindly. Just be sure that any decision to part ways with a mentor is truly based on their inability to get you where you want to be and not a knee-jerk reaction to a bruised ego.

As with everything else, the success of this relationship depends on your ability to be curious, open, and ready to evolve.

CHAPTER SIX

NEW HABITS,
NEW LIFE

DID YOU KNOW you have about 85,000 individual thoughts every single day?

And did you know about 95% of those thoughts are the exact same thoughts you had yesterday?

It's true. Take a minute to think back through the last few days. Are there any thoughts that passed through your mind every single day? Maybe thoughts about:

- How you felt when your alarm went off?
- What you were going to eat for breakfast?
- What time it was when you left the house?

- The work waiting for you at the office?
- Traffic on your commute?
- Having to deal with a difficult employee?
- Your lunch plans?
- Your dinner plans?
- All the things you didn't get done that day?
- Your relationship with your spouse?
- Challenges with your kids?
- The future of your company?

We tend to let our minds run on autopilot. Because of this, we get locked into the same routine day in, day out. Every morning, you wake up thinking, "Ugh, I have so much work to do today." This dread is what keeps you in bed until the last minute, which accounts for the fact that you arrive at work hungry, which accounts for the fact that every challenge that confronts you feels huge, confusing, and chaotic.

Bottom line: you keep wishing your life would change, but you do nothing to change it.

Now, you may not see it this way. It's possible—even likely— that you've actually taken some big, bold swings in your career. Whether it was a home run or a miss, you're still here reading this book. So you have to wonder, why didn't that big change stick?

I'll tell you why. It was an attempt at a quick fix. You can bring on new investors, open a new branch, or take a chance on an innovative new product. But if your mind is still locked into the same 85,000 thoughts and the same daily habits, there is no way you are going to be able to fundamentally change your business, your life, or yourself.

It may feel counterintuitive, but you have to start small.

Choose the Right Habits

First, figure out what needs to change in your day-to-day routine. Sit down for a quick brainstorm. Ask yourself questions like:

How could I change my morning routine to help me find a more active mindset for the day?

What could I do when I arrive at work to make sure I don't spend the day putting out fires? How will I decide when I can delegate and when I can handle a problem myself?

When will I give myself mental breaks during the day, and how will I use those opportunities?

What can I do in the evening to rest and recharge in preparation for tomorrow?

Don't worry, you won't have to put all these ideas into action. At least not all at once. Right now, you're just considering new habits.

Things like:

> *I could drink a glass of water to rehydrate and energize as soon as I get up.*

> *I could go for a morning jog.*

> *I could take one employee out for lunch every week as a way to get to know my team better.*

> *Before I got home at the end of the day, I could prepare my to-do list for tomorrow so I don't allow unexpected obstacles to derail my priorities.*

You get the idea.

As you consider developing new habits, remember that this is about creating habits that align with your goals.

You are not trying to eliminate bad habits.

Why not?

Well, it's a mindset thing. Drinking a glass of water first thing in the morning accomplishes roughly the same thing as drinking less caffeine. But the mindset is different. If your goal is to get hydrated right away, you are actively building a better life. When you build that habit, you succeed. But if your goal is to cut back on coffee, you're just trying to make your life less bad. The best you can do is not fail.

Remember, what you focus on grows. If you want to promote a spirit of creativity and self-improvement, you need to focus on creation and self-improvement.

Plus, eliminating a bad habit is much, much harder than cultivating a good habit. Just hang in there and be patient. As you build a more intentional routine, those bad habits fade away.

How to Build a Habit: The Compounding Effect

You may be aware of Warren Buffet's famous advice for investors. He is a huge advocate for turning small investments into major gains through the magic of compound interest. It makes sense. You earn interest on your interest, and the longer you allow your investment to build interest, the faster you build wealth. In the end, that small investment often pays better than a larger, bolder, riskier investment.

It works the exact same way when you build new habits. If you start with one small, sustainable habit, that new habit makes it easier to make two more slightly larger changes, which pave the way for four, eight, sixteen new habits.

On the other hand, if you started by trying to make sixteen big changes all at once, you would likely fail to keep any of them up. Maybe one, at *best*.

Take a minute to look back at the list of new habits you'd like to cultivate. I'd be willing to bet there is something on that list you have already tried to do. Maybe you already tried waking up an hour earlier for a workout. It went well for the first three days, then you slipped up after a night of working late, you fell out of the routine, and you couldn't get back in the groove. Or you *did* institute a weekly meeting with all your department heads, but a few scheduling conflicts ultimately derailed the effort.

If this is the case, this is a good time to remember that you are no longer going to live in the past. Your failure to form a specific habit in the past has nothing to do with your ability to create that same habit in the future. Why? Because that failure has nothing to do with who you are. It's a matter of how you approached your goal.

You need to start small. Very small. So small that it feels ridiculous.

Begin with an inconsequential change. If you brush your teeth with your right hand, set an intention to start brushing with your left for two weeks. If you put on your watch before you put on your shoes, do the opposite.

Do these changes do anything to make your life better? Not directly, no.

But they train your mind to see yourself as changeable. If you decide to create a habit of putting on your left shoe before your right shoe, you will succeed. And if you forget one morning, it's not a problem. That slip-up will not register to your mind as a failure. It won't make you think you're incapable of putting your left shoe on first. You will read the situation for what it is: a mistake. The next morning, you'll get it right. Once this change becomes a habit, your mind thinks, "Huh. I guess I *can* change a little." That success makes it easier to add a new change... one that matters a little more. This is the Compounding Effect.

Now, let's say you start with something bigger. You want to do thirty minutes of cold calling every morning, even though you hate cold calling. You sit down at your desk, remind yourself that you can master cold sales, and dial. It's thirty minutes of pure anxiety, and you can't bring yourself to do it again the next day. Guess what your self-protective mind tells you?

> "You'll never be able to do this. It's not who you are. Trying to change will only make you miserable."

This is why we start with changes that don't matter and work our way up to the ones that do.

So, pick something tiny that does not matter in the least.

Then try making another tiny adjustment that matters a little. You can refer back to your list from the previous exercise, but if you do, break off a small piece of a larger habit. If your goal is to take a morning jog, start with a jog to the end of the block.

Building positive habits is like building clarity. You need to be patient and you need to celebrate the small victories. Trust me. They add up to huge wins over time.

CHAPTER SEVEN

FUEL
YOUR GOALS

I CAN USUALLY gauge a new franchisee's potential for success the moment I first meet them. It's not that I can tell whether or not they have "It." It has nothing to do with their firm handshake or winning smile... at least, not exactly.

It's all about their energy.

Are they slow or alert? Well-rested or worn down? Curious and engaged or just trying to get through the day?

A business owner who is energetic and alert has unlimited potential. A lethargic business owner can *maybe* hope to keep their business alive *at best*.

Now, if you're like a lot of business owners, you may think of energy as a luxury. After all, your job is difficult and demanding. You wake up each morning with a mile-long to-do list. You deal with emotionally draining challenges like angry customers and employee conflicts. Then you go home and try to be fully present for your family. You try to be a best friend for your spouse and a patient guide for your children. Odds are, you stay up later than you intended. When your alarm goes off in the morning, it's not your ambition that gets you out of bed, but the crushing responsibility of providing for a family and succeeding just enough to make sure your employees can provide for *their* families.

Of course you'd love to sleep better, eat better, and exercise more. But a person in your position just doesn't have that luxury, right?

It may be true that you're not at a point in your career where you can afford luxuries.

But health and energy are not luxuries.

You must take care of your body. You will not make it as a business owner if you don't. It's not just about having the fuel you need to get things done. Your energy level directly affects your mindset.

If you're a parent, you know this all too well. Your kid throws a tantrum over screen time. You hold your ground. They scream louder. If it were 10:00 a.m. on a Saturday, you might take a breath and try to come up with a creative way to handle this conflict without rewarding their behavior. But it's not 10:00 a.m. on a Saturday. It's 7:00 p.m. on a Thursday, and you're exhausted. So you give in. You hate giving in. You wish you weren't giving in. But your conviction is not as powerful as your need for silence and rest.

When you work towards transforming your mindset, you learn to believe in your own potential. You nurture passion for your work and a razor-sharp focus on your purpose. If you pair that with a strong, energetic body, you can do anything. But if you neglect physical self-care, your focus blurs. You are no longer alert, passionate, and creative. You are just sort of... getting through the day. Nothing has really changed.

If your goal is to truly adopt a new mindset, you have to take care of your body.

Active Body, Active Mind

If you don't exercise, it's time to start.

If you exercise sporadically, it's time to schedule regular, non-negotiable workouts.

If you're already physically active, great! Keep it up.

At this phase, "exercise" doesn't have to mean a full-blown workout. You don't have to hit the gym or run ten miles a day.

Instead, ask yourself, *"How can I add movement to my daily routine?"* Movement can mean many different things, and you're likely to find some form of physical activity you enjoy. You could go for a bike ride, swim, dance, or even just start with a morning walk. Right now, you're just trying to move more than you did before. That's easy enough, right?

Exercise not only helps you stay fit and energetic, but it also:

- Reduces stress, anxiety, and depression
- Helps you sleep better
- Stimulates chemicals that improve brain function and memory
- Boosts your immunity
- Builds endurance

Every single benefit on that list is going to help you build a more successful career.

So, make a commitment right now to make movement a regular routine. Now, there are a few rules for this commitment.

- Decide when you are going to exercise and mark it on your calendar. Choose a time when you are least likely to become distracted by other obligations. If possible, schedule your movement at the exact same time every single day. Consistency helps.
- Tell anyone who needs to know that you are not available at this time.

- Start small. If you don't already have a workout routine, begin with a ten-minute walk and build up over time. If you already exercise for ninety minutes whenever you have free time, make a commitment to workout for thirty minutes every day.

You know the drill by now. You need to make it as easy as possible to succeed at keeping this promise to yourself. In fact, a regular movement routine is one of the best ways to increase your sense of self-worth. When you follow-through on a commitment to take better care of your body, you tell yourself you're worth it.

You're worth waking up a little earlier. You're worth the sweat.

You're worth your own investment.

Eat to Win

Does your diet provide fuel for the day or just drag you down?

When you load up on sugar, fried foods, and drinks after work, you burden your body with the task of protecting itself. You force your system to channel all its energy into processing harmful ingredients and filtering toxins. And you still feel awful in the process. Sugar and caffeine make you crash and burn. Fatty foods make digestion slow and uncomfortable. The inflammatory effects of alcohol can follow you into the next day, even when you drink in moderation.

What you eat matters. It's not just about health and longevity (though those are both good enough reasons to eat well.) If you truly want to excel in your field, you have to fuel for excellence.

Now, you can do a deep dive on nutrition and come up with a long list of foods to eat and foods to avoid. You will find arguments for eating organic foods only, committing to a raw diet, or consuming exclusively whole foods. Deciding which of these complicated diets is best for you... well, that's a job for Future You. That's something you can worry about when you've mastered healthy eating and are ready to kick things up a notch.

Right now, your only goal is sustainable, incremental change.

Make a list of the foods you eat most frequently. Look for opportunities to make small adjustments. A few examples:

- If you head for the coffee machine first thing in the morning, drink a green juice or a glass of water with lime first. You don't have to drop coffee altogether, but you are likely to need less of it if you prioritize hydration and nutrition.
- If you get a candy bar from the vending machine to pep yourself up every afternoon, try a walk instead. Movement actually gives you a better energy boost than sugar does.

- Eat lighter by making small adjustments to your meal habits. Mix in more greens and stop when you feel full, even if it means packing away leftovers.

Again, choose one, sustainable change and build a healthier life from there.

Your Daily Routine

Finally, I strongly recommend working towards a morning routine that helps you get both body and mind in shape for the day. My own routine looks like this:

- Before I even get out of bed, I take three or five minutes to appreciate the things I have. This often includes things like good health, a loving family, fulfilling work, etc.
- As soon as I get up, I wash my face with cold water.
- I do some simple physical activity to raise my pulse for two minutes.
- Instead of going straight for the coffee, I drink a green juice or water with lime.
- I do about two minutes of deep breathing, followed by ten minutes of stretching (usually outside).

I also do not touch my phone for at least thirty minutes after waking up. I highly recommend you establish your own no-phone policy first thing in the morning. Whether you're checking social media or scrolling through emails, your phone offers myriad distractions from your purpose and goals. In order to ensure an effective morning routine, you must be fully in control of the thoughts and ideas that launch your day.

You may have noticed that nothing about this routine is remotely challenging. And yet, I credit these morning rituals with helping me prepare for a productive, energetic day.

Washing my face with cold water wakes me up and stimulates blood circulation.

The moment of appreciation establishes alignment between my brain and my heart so I can approach my day with an awareness of what really matters to me. This routine also helps me immediately focus on the people I care about and the life I have built, reminding me that I have already found a way to live a fulfilling life. If I've done it before, I can do it again today.

By drinking juice and doing deep breathing exercises first, I make sure I get my body into an alkaline state before introducing the acidity of coffee. (Translation: I avoid inflammation and feel better.)

Each of these tasks is complete in a matter of minutes, but they prepare me to be alert, focused, and energized all day long. Find a morning routine that does the same thing for you.

CHAPTER EIGHT

WELCOME TO YOUR NEW WAY OF LIFE

WHEN YOU CHANGE your mindset, you change your life... not just because you discover a perspective that allows you to become more successful, but because your entire life is now about ongoing transformation.

Remember, your goal is not to reach a specific level of success. Not yet. Right now, your goal is to progress through the blueprint for growth I shared in Chapter Three. By the final stage, you are a Creator. You are someone who sees your life, your business, and your world as changeable, and you are changeable within it. You are someone who looks for opportunities to learn and improve, in good times and bad.

Evolving as a person is no longer a task you have to endure to get to the next step. It's a way of life.

Does this state of constant transformation sound exhausting?

It's actually not. Routine is exhausting. Spending a decade stuck in the same rut with the same worries is exhausting. But constant exploration and growth... that's exciting. Your new lifestyle is fun and energizing. Best of all, it's fulfilling, even when you're not at your most successful.

Here's why.

You Transform as a Human Being

As a goal-oriented entrepreneur, you may have a habit of seeing personal growth as a project with a finite timeline and a target result. You want to become a more organized professional, so you read a book on time management, you create a new filing system, and you download an app to keep you on track.

That's it. Now you're more organized. You're done.

That's the fantasy. It's not the reality. If your goal is to become more organized, you're probably going to do all those things, then forget to use the app or discover that the new filing system isn't really any better than your old one. You made external changes to achieve a single desired result, and in the end, you only "changed" for a week or two.

This process of transforming your mindset opens up a lifelong routine of continuous growth. You don't just "get organized." You cultivate inner clarity and focus as you work towards improving your external procedures and systems. Little by little, *you become an organized person*—not just in terms of what you do, but in terms of the way you think about storing information, managing time, and communicating with your staff.

During this process of growth, you graduate from Victim to Hopeful, or from Hopeful to Believer.

Then, when you realize it's time to get serious about marketing, you no longer see "marketing skills" as a checklist of courses you should take or specialists you should hire. Instead, you look within for clues about the beliefs that have been holding you back until this point.

Maybe you're "bad at marketing" because you don't consider yourself to be very creative. Maybe advertising feels slimy to you. Maybe deep down, marketing yourself means opening yourself up to failure and disappointment.

As you work to break free from these limiting beliefs and take practical steps towards building a better marking plan, you begin to transform from the inside. Over time, you start to see yourself as a business owner who can bring in buyers.

You even begin to notice this pattern of regular transformation in your personal life. You get in an argument with your spouse and start thinking, *"How can I become a better partner because of this argument? Am I really hearing her? Could I be more empathetic?"* You become more patient with your children. You become more compassionate in your friendships.

You're not just building a business you can be proud of. You are becoming a human being who is worthy of your own esteem and admiration.

You Have a Wider Impact on the World

When you began this journey, you probably wanted one thing:

To build a better, more profitable business.

But because personal growth begins with identifying your deeper purpose and desires, you gradually begin to see a much bigger picture. You are no longer trying to "double the size of your team." You are in search of new talent to help you move forward in your mission to serve your clients better. Now, customer reviews are a means for celebrating your staff or finding opportunities to help your buyers find more peace of mind in the midst of a property disaster. Instead of pushing your team to be more productive, you inspire them to be more creative, which helps them discover a deeper level of fulfillment in their work.

In other words, you begin to see how your growth benefits everyone.

Plus, when you approach each day with energy, focus, and passion, that positivity radiates out to those around you. Customers are eager to work with you. Employees are inspired to emulate you. Your family feels more valued and appreciated by you.

When you change yourself, you change the world.

You Discover New Capabilities

Finally, your growth mindset guarantees you will develop skills you haven't even dreamed of yet.

When I began my own journey, I was focused on one thing: fixing the stutter.

When I did fix my stutter—essentially succeeding at something I had always believed was impossible—I wondered if I could stretch myself further and become a more confident public speaker.

For me, diving into public speaking meant giving a presentation at our company convention. The more I spoke before our franchisees, the more I saw myself as a mentor and motivator for business owners.

Now I've written books. I've developed a training app and created an online community of bold business owners with big plans.

When I attempted my first staff meeting at 911 Restoration, I wasn't thinking about becoming a thought leader. All I wanted was to speak in smoother sentences.

But growth is a snowball rolling down a hill. It gets faster. It gets bigger.

This is the Compounding Effect. It doesn't matter how small you start. Just start.

⬦ Exercise: Dream Big

Throughout this book, I've encouraged you to let go of old, self-limiting beliefs. I've encouraged you to recognize that you're limitless... that you can do and be anything you want as long as you're open to growth.

If you're like a lot of people, you probably have trouble grasping the full meaning of "limitless" in the context of your own life. In fact, when you sat down to read this book, you were probably in the kind of headspace where you'd be content to just make a little more money so you can enjoy more financial security or have more time with your family. You weren't necessarily trying to conquer the industry.

But that is exactly why I love teaching business owners how to cultivate a growth mindset. When they first come to me, they are—above all else—afraid of failing. Once their mindset changes, they are no longer driven by fear. They are driven by possibility.

Even if you're not there yet, take a moment to imagine yourself as limitless. Really imagine it. In fact, write it down. Take out a sheet of paper and ask yourself, *"If I really were limitless…"*

"Who would I want to become?"
"How would I like to influence the world?"
"What skills would I like to develop? What bold professional moves would I like to make?"

Try to imagine the absolute best case scenario. If your first instinct is to say, "I'd like to discover more clarity as a leader," consider something more extreme, like, "I'd like to be the kind of boss who always knows exactly what to do in a crisis."

Focus on:

- Who you can become
- What you can create

We're not talking about buying a Bugatti or winning awards.

No, we're taking a moment to reflect on the expansive potential of your ever-evolving self.

Even if you're not ready to believe in great things, give yourself this one small moment to imagine them.

CHAPTER NINE

THE NEW
YOU

LOOK AROUND YOU. Notice where you are in life, how you feel, what you value, what you fear, what you hope for. Remember this time in your life, because you are going to look back on this as the moment when everything changed. This is when you begin a journey of baby steps that will ultimately lead to the realization of all those dreams you now think of as "unlikely."

I mean it. No other change you make in your life will be as impactful as changing your mindset.

Of course, this also means no other change will be as challenging or as complicated. After all the ground we just covered, you may be feeling a little lost. How do you apply all these ideas to your life? Where do you even begin?

Let me offer a few guidelines to get you started.

Begin Today

The first step is both simple and crucial.

Begin by making a commitment to yourself today. Right now. Set down this book, find a sticky note, and literally put your commitment in writing.

> I commit to growth.

Now remember, this is a life-changing commitment, but it's going to work because your *only* focus is growth. This is not a commitment to losing twenty pounds or making two million dollars next year. You are simply saying that each day (and eventually each moment), you are going to do something to shift your mindset and evolve as a person. That's it.

Having said that, it is absolutely crucial that you stick to this commitment. The first and most effective way to cultivate self-trust is by keeping the promises you make to yourself.

How Does the New You Handle This Situation?

Next, practice thinking through your daily challenges with a growth mindset. Start with a difficult situation you're facing right now. Ask yourself:

How would the New Me handle this situation?

Remember:

- The New You looks for opportunities to learn, improve, and create.
- The New You acts with intention instead of *re*acting in fear.
- The New You is energetic and clear-headed.
- The New You knows that self-limiting beliefs are lies based on your upbringing, social influences, or painful life experiences.
- The New You is certain of your ability to design the life you want.

When you find yourself worrying over a problem in your work or your life, take a moment to imagine what the New You would do. This exercise is important not just because it guides you toward more intentional, meaningful choices, but also because it trains your mind to start reasoning through your challenges differently.

Take the first step right now. Try examining a current problem through the perspective of the New You. How does that change the way you deal with the issue? And what will you do with this new perspective?

You may struggle with this exercise at first. Don't give up and don't be too hard on yourself. Remember, you don't see your mindset as a system of beliefs; you see it as reality. Thinking differently is going to take practice. Keep following the exercises in this book to train your mind in new perspectives. It will get easier in time.

How Does the New You Start the Day?

I cannot emphasize how important it is to create a mindful morning routine. Take a moment right now to decide what you need to do when you first wake up to get yourself focused and alert, physically and mentally.

Ask yourself:

- How can I add a little movement to my morning routine?
- How can I nourish my body so it feels strong and supported?
- What can I do to put myself in a compassionate and creative headspace?

You can refer back to my routine in Chapter Seven if you need a few ideas. As you design your own morning ritual, remember to keep it fairly short. If you have to wake up an hour earlier to get it all in, you won't be able to keep it up.

Start by making better choices about how to use the time you already have. Once you have your new routine in place, you can think about challenging yourself to wake up earlier.

You may also want to build your new daily routine one piece at a time. For example, you might begin by taking a moment of appreciation before you get out of bed tomorrow morning. Do this every morning for the next couple weeks.

Once this feels like a natural part of your morning routine, add the next step. Maybe it's some light stretching or drinking a full glass of water. In time, you'll build a sustainable and impactful daily ritual.

Nurturing Your Growth Mindset Over the Long Term

As you continue on your path from Victim to Creator, remember the central principles of a growth mindset.

- Your perception of a situation reflects your state of mind, not reality.
- Your beliefs come from a complex history of outside influences and personal experience. They are not based in truth.
- You are not the things you own, the accomplishments you have achieved, or the talents you have.
- You are limitless because of your ability to change.
- Embracing your full potential means choosing to live an active and creative life instead of reacting to fears. *You* are in control.

- In order to get in touch with your true purpose and deeper goals, you must cultivate clarity within.
- You are responsible for fueling that clarity with a healthy, active body.

Some of these ideas may already be part of your belief system. Others may take a while to fully internalize. Much like the journey to business success, the process of transforming your mindset can not be graphed as a steadily ascending line. You will stumble, slip, and backtrack. That's okay. Just keep going. I have organized this book so you can easily review any topic as you need to. And you will need to.

I have also provided two supplemental sections at the back of this book: a blueprint to get you started on your journey and a list of resources to help you over the long term.

Finally, I'd like to congratulate you on completing this book. By doing so, you have already shown yourself that you can follow through on a commitment to growth. Take a moment to feel this success... and let this small change inspire the next.

BUILDING YOUR NEW MINDSET: A BLUEPRINT

MY HOPE IS that you can use the ideas I shared in this book to build a strategy for mindset transformation according to your own strengths and weaknesses.

Having said that, I know the concepts I shared are complex and a bit more abstract than the typical tips for entrepreneurs. In the interest of simplifying things, I'm providing a blueprint to help you get started. This blueprint is designed with business owners in mind. It's simple, straight-forward, and easy to implement while managing a busy and ever-changing schedule.

Define Your Future Self

Block out some time to sit down and think about who you want to become. If the answer doesn't come easily, ask yourself questions like:

- What kind of impact do you want to make on the world?
- What aspects of your life today will matter the most to you when you are eighty years old?
- Who do you want to become as a person and as a leader?
- What kind of legacy do you hope to build?
- What type of role model do you want to be for your family?
- How do you want your employees and customers to feel when they work with you?
- What is your greater purpose?

If the answer still doesn't come easily, that's okay. Choose something simple but true, like "I want to become a better communicator," or "I want to become a more confident leader." In time, your larger ambitions will become clearer. (Refer to Chapter Four for a refresher on building mental clarity.) For now, just find a small dream to start with.

Change Your Habits

Block out some time to brainstorm and list the positive habits you need to cultivate in order to become the person you wish to be. You can refer to Chapter Six for a review of how to choose and build new habits. If you just need a quick recap, here are a couple checklists to use as a guide.

Consider habits relating to:

- Morning routine
- Daily movement
- Nutrition
- Time management
- Communication

Remember to:

- Focus on cultivating *good* habits instead of trying to stop *bad* habits.
- Choose habits that you can realistically adopt in the near future. (In other words, start with adding more greens to your diet instead of going full-on vegan.)
- Set a plan for starting with one inconsequential change, then *gradually* adding more meaningful habits into your lifestyle. Remember, you are *compounding* success, not trying to transform your life overnight.
- Commit to making the first small change. Start immediately and start ferociously.

Change Your Thinking

As you work through your strategy of gradually cultivating habits that are more aligned with the person you want to become, practice *thinking* like your Future Self as well. With each new situation you encounter, take a minute to ask yourself how the New You would handle it.

In other words, how would you approach this challenge if you truly believed you were capable of using it to move closer to your goals?

When you have the answer, do what your Future Self would do.

Heighten Your Self-Awareness

At the end of each day, take some time to reflect on a situation you handled using your old Victim mentality. Ask yourself:

- What fear were you reacting to?
- What ingrained belief made you feel like there was only one way to approach that situation?
- How would the New You approach this situation differently?

Don't beat yourself up for not acting in a Creator mentality every time. That's not what this exercise is about. Instead, embrace this as an opportunity to practice flexible thinking. The more you do this, the better you become at considering alternative approaches in the moment.

Practice Appreciation

Finally, train your mind to focus on the good. The defining characteristic of a Creator is the steadfast belief in one's own ability to create the life they want, no matter what obstacles may arise. This requires positive thinking, and positive thinking is a muscle you have to train.

Take 3-5 minutes at the beginning and end of each day to remember the things you are grateful for. Don't just scroll through a mental list... "my health, my family, my new all-terrain tires..."

Give yourself time to imagine each item. Think of your daughter's smiling face. Remember how much you were able to accomplish today with your strong and able body. Imagine the pine smell of the mountain air as you explore rough roads with your new tires. Don't just count your blessings, *feel* blessed. Experience genuine appreciation.

The more you do this, the easier it becomes to see that joy and fulfillment are not only within your grasp; you've already claimed some of it for yourself.

If you're going through a particularly difficult time, this exercise may feel impossible or even frustrating at first. Stick with it anyway. Gratitude can blossom even in the worst of circumstances, and when you live with appreciation, you find yourself attracting more opportunities to thrive.

I'll say it one more time:

> What you focus on grows.

While your mindset transformation will one day extend well beyond the simple steps of this blueprint, the strategy I just laid out is more than enough to get you started.

Ready to dig deeper? Read on for recommended resources.

RESOURCES FOR THE JOURNEY

I WROTE THIS book to serve as a quick guide for busy entrepreneurs. Now that you've learned the basic concepts of cultivating a growth mindset, you may find that you'd like to go deeper or even just have a little more support through the day-to-day challenges of running a business.

I've got you covered.

Further Reading

Get Out of the Truck: Build the Business You Always Dreamed About by **Idan Shpizear**

This book provides clear, step-by-step guidance on leadership and strategy. It's perfect for current business owners as well as aspiring entrepreneurs.

Leadershift: The 11 Essential Changes Every Leader Must Embrace by John C. Maxwell

This book is packed with wisdom to support your career-long transformation as an ever-innovating, continuously advancing business leader.

Meditation Resources

I strongly recommend mediation as a technique for building clarity and developing a mindset of cultivation. There are countless free resources out there to guide you as you build your meditation practice, but I am an especially big fan of Dr. Joe Dispenza's morning and evening meditations. You can find these guided meditations pretty easily with an Internet search.

Join Our Community for Ongoing Support

For both practical tips and motivating insights, join the community at GetOutOfTheTruck.life. Here, you can sign up for my newsletter, connect with other business owners, and discover fresh content designed to guide you through the challenges of running a business. This site also connects you with essential business solutions like back office resources and one-on-one marketing consultations. Finally, I invite you to join the Get Out of the Truck group on Facebook for ongoing discussion with me and with your colleagues.

I created the Get Out of the Truck community with the goal of helping new, aspiring, and struggling business owners finally make the mental transition from tradesperson to business owner. This community exists to serve you, and I am always here to offer support, answer questions, and celebrate your successes—large and small—as you become the New You.

I wish you all the best in your journey. Please let me know how I can help.

www.ingramcontent.com/pod-product-compliance
Lightning Source LLC
Chambersburg PA
CBHW061150040426
42445CB00013B/1635